New Forest
reflections

For Marian

New Forest
reflections

Rosemary & Dan Powell

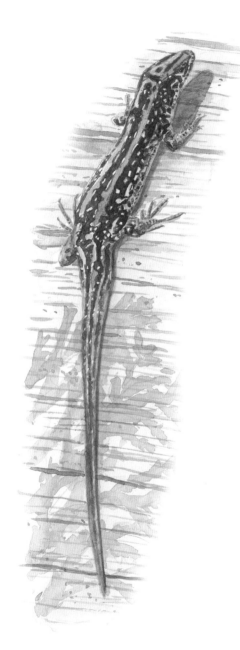

First published November 2015
Rosemary & Dan Powell
4 Forth Close
Hillhead
Hampshire
PO14 3SZ

ISBN 978-0-9572301-2-5

Printed by InPrint www.inprintlitho.com

Sand Lizard - left. Redstart - opposite.

Contents

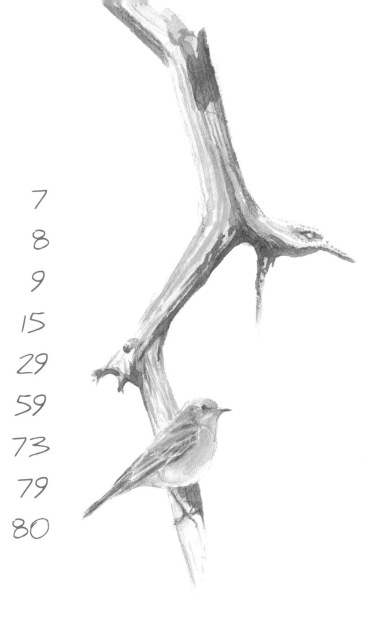

NIGHTSING - NATOR + DAN POWELL

Foreword

Away from roads, lanes and camp sites, the New Forest is a place of quiet beauty and eloquent loneliness. It is an area of navigational challenge, at times serious. Those who accept this challenge may find themselves in winter with patrolling hen harriers and busy hawfinches and in summer with Dartford warblers harshly calling from the gorse, with marauding peregrine falcons above and during twilight, ghostly nightjars endlessly churring. Careful visitors will find deer in numbers, spectacular and obvious in the rutting season of the autumn. The choice of reptiles is of the best to the careful observer; sand lizards have been re-introduced with success; a male viper sunning itself quietly in May is a delight to see. Speckled wood butterflies, aggressive to one another, abound in the woodland and the beautiful but tiny green hairstreak on heathland can make the day. Territorial four-spot dragonflies along extensive damp areas are eye-catching. The deciduous trees of the forest are nature's architecture. The bark of the trees is often covered in numerous shapely lichens and beneath the trees in autumn the Forest shows a remarkable array of fungi on its floor especially the red-capped, white-spotted but poisonous fly agaric.

For many years now Dan and Rosemary Powell together have graced with many paintings and illustrations our knowledge of the wildlife of many parts of this world but especially of Hampshire. Always they have conveyed their enjoyment for us, the viewers and readers, with care, great skill and taste to reflect their own love of all elements of natural history. I am honoured to write this preface for their own reflections of this special and favoured place in their home county.

Commander Tony Norris FRGS

Green hairstreak - above.
Nightjars - opposite.

Map

Ashley Walk
Leaden Hall
Bramshaw Commons

Hyde Common
Eyeworth Pond

Holly Hatch
Woodford Bottom

Ashurst

Lyndhurst

Ringwood

Denny Wood
Bishop'sDyke

Pignall inclosure

Brockenhurst

Beaulieu Heath

Lymington

Introduction

Beginnings

As a 1960's nipper a trip to the Forest meant a family day out. A seemingly never ending car journey was punctuated every five minutes with an enquiry 'are we there yet'? The day culminated in a picnic and game of footy. However I seem to remember my older brothers speaking of crossbill, Dartford warbler and in hushed tones, honey buzzard. Meaningless to me at the time, but something must have sunk in. Once the teenage angst was over, these words began to take on meaning and the Forest became a must place to go birdwatching. Cadging lifts from unsuspecting friends, my then vitally important bird list began to build. Notebooks were filled with lists of birds seen and gradually scribblings crept into the margins.

Glanville fritillary - above. A rare butterfly found on the Isle of Wight, but for now it has a finger-hold New Forest population.

Acres Down in spring - left.

Little did I know that in a parallel world, Rosie had spent time here as well. Taking holidays with her family during the 1970's, sowing the seeds for the future.

'...I remember the ponies causing moments of fun, when they would come around poking their heads through the door of the caravan to share our breakfast. How little things have changed, now they hope to share D's. pasty or custard doughnut. No chance there then...'

Today we can be there after a half hour wrestle with the motorway, ready to explore.

'The time will some day arrive when as England becomes more and more overcrowded – as each heath and common are swallowed up - the New Forest will be as much a necessity to the country as the parks are now to London'.

J.R.Wise – The New Forest, Its History and Scenery (1863).

This equally applies to the Forest today.

Reflections

It's all about somewhere that we share, a place we retreat to when we can - moments grasped between the dead-lines of work. In a county with increasing pressure on its open spaces, the Forest still has room to wander in and at times lose ourselves.

We haven't attempted to put together a comprehensive guide to New Forest wildlife. It would be a huge book just to scratch the surface of what can be found and there are many worthy tomes already written. It simply focuses on; a small number of many visits made during the Forest seasons, the things we encounter that inspire us and our reflections of them in images and words.

Sometimes we go with knowledge aforehand searching for something in particular, with varying degrees of success. Sometimes we stick a pin in the map and explore. Othertimes it is just an escape from the noise of an impatient world. Either way once in the Forest we switch-off from the rest of the world and mooch.

Most of the places are described as the day unfolded. A few are based on a combination of visits, making it appear as if we had a very good day indeed, these are used to show just how rich some sites are.

The Forest is an unpredictable beast, often rewarding our efforts, though at times it can feel as if everything has scarpered. Those days are the ones when you make the most of watching wood pigeons or you quickly succumb to the lure of a bowl of hot soup and a flagon of frothing ale.

The artworks come in three flavours; those made on the spot in sketchbooks and scraps of watercolour paper, those started in the field and developed later at home and those created back in the studio, based on sketches, photos and where the brushes take us.

Early sketching effort. From my twitching years - above.
Homy Ridge in autumn - left.

Gladiolus. The one flower that would be missed, if the Forest ceased to exist.
Hurst Spit in winter.
Porkers & fungus - opposite.

The texts are more of a challenge. Most are random thoughts scribbled down as a field-diary and represented as faithfully as we dare, keeping them close to our emotions of the moment. Others are more considered and hopefully informative.

As mentioned earlier, a little research beforehand can point you towards the things you would like to see. In some cases books can change the way you look at the Forest. Clive Chatters' book on New Forest flora is one of those, it has helped us appreciate how the Forest with its mosaic of habitats works as a whole. It is also a good read, although Rosie's eyes have occasionally turned skyward at my excited mention of an interesting sedge to be found in the middle of a bog.

With experience you will instinctively pick out clues to finding the wildlife. For example, a well managed heath has a patchwork of heather at different stages of growth. Mature domed shaped heather with a stand of mature gorse, are the best places to listen out for Dartford warblers. You will also quickly work out where dry heath changes to wet heath and bog!

What's in the name?

History tells us that the New Forest was formed by William 1 in 1079. In those times the term 'forest' simply described areas where the law of the land and forest law had to be obeyed, not a woodland as we think of it today. At nearly a thousand years old, it cannot really be considered 'new' either.

With a low population, a large tract of furzey waste and close proximity to William's capital city of Winchester, this corner of Hampshire was ideal for creating his new forest hunting ground. Once designated as a forest a harsh regime to protect the King's timber and venison gripped the local people. One of the only concessions given was permission to graze their livestock on the open forest. And so the shape of the landscape as we know it began to emerge.

Today the New Forest is one of Britains smallest National Parks. With a growing population on its doorstep the pressures on it are huge. The balance between protecting the internationally important wildlife that lives there and providing a place of recreation and relaxation for the numerous visitors, is and will continue to be a complex one to maintain.

Redstarts, scarlet elf cup, lichens, tawny owl, gladiolus & holly blue on blackberry - left to right.

'Clear of main roads which cut inelegantly across it, away from busy car parks, noisy caravan and camping sites, there lies the quiet majesty of the New Forest, a relic of the days when Norman sovereigns sequestered areas of woodland and heaths for their own interests of hunting deer. Ordinary folk were often excluded. A few remained as 'commoners', permitted to graze domestic stock as they still do. The New Forest is also a relic of the ancient naval ship building industry; oak trees were cut and replacement saplings were planted to provide in places now the majestic but ordered and often serried ranks of trees. To be with ancient oaks and beech trees, perhaps 300 and 400 years of age and more, is to be in the presence of the 'lordly ones'.

Recently, it was a place for the practice of conifer forestry and now it is a National Park being recovered to a natural state and to be enjoyed with care by many people. In places, its borders run along the north shore of the western Solent with splendid access, superb views across to the Isle of Wight and a variety of seabirds breeding and offshore. Altogether, the New Forest with its variety is a joy'.   Tony Norris (2015).

Great grey shrike. Most years 2-3 birds can be found gracing the winter landscapes of the Forest. Their striking grey, black and white plumage is a pleasure to paint, but its dapper dress belies a fearsome owner that hunts over large areas in search of small birds. They are fittingly known as the butcher bird - a title gained from their habit of creating larders of prey impaled on thorny branches.

GREAT GREY SHRIKE -
I.P. WOODFORD BOTTOM

Early Spring

A Woodford wander

A favourite area of ours to explore in search of signs of spring.

'...The old birder's adage goes along the lines of "find the pipits and there be the shrike". I can't remember it ever paying off. I much prefer. "Hello there. Have you come to see our shrike? It's normally over there, perched in the third pine from the left in the boggy bit". We hadn't really, but were delighted to watch the shrike, in the third pine from the left in the boggy bit. If only it always went like that.

Wandering on we picked up on a herd of red deer spread across the hillside. Going into stealth mode for a closer view, we were distracted by a roe buck watching us from a stand of pines in the middle of the bog. Nicely distracted, we were then drawn to a small herd of fallow does crashing disorientedly through the mire. Not bad, three species of deer in one vista. Back to the stalking - downwind, good, keeping in the cover of the gorse, good... Hey what's that chap in the bright turquoise shorts up to? Don't walk there. Can't he see them? He didn't, nor did he seem to care and evidently neither did the deer care about him. Not as timid as we thought they might be.

There were mainly hinds in the group, but two stood out as being young stags. One having had a better hair day than the other, with antlers full of heather. This debris is collected as the stags sweep their antlers across the heather in order to strengthen the neck muscles, in readiness for the rigours of the autumn rut...'

15

16

'...onto Hasley Inclosure. Groups of finches scattered in front of us and a herd of fallow does, watched nervously through a veil of tangled pine branches. A chiffchaff sang. Lesser celandine and common dog violet were now in bloom.

Back on the heath a male wheatear stood proud announcing his arrival from his African winter quarters. Making short flights flashing its white rump, that realised its Saxon name of white-arse. A name later refined to wheatear by the prudish Victorians...'

A peacock loafs in the sun - opposite. Wary fallow does - above. Lesser celandine - below. Cheeky seven-spot ladybird, moving the hands forward an hour on the town hall clock or moschatel, at Blashford Lakes - middle. Cladonia floerkeana, a lichen - top.

'...The vast landscapes of the Forest grab your attention, yet taking the time to look down can be equally arresting. Whole landscapes in miniature, revealed amongst the mosses and lichens...'

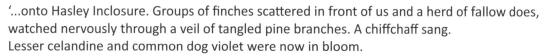

'...Just when we were convinced that spring was well on the way, a male hen harrier drifted on easy wings across the view. Reminding us that winter may well still have a bite...' - left.

Roe buck - top. Heath dog-violets - above.

Common dog violets - above.
Wheatear - left.
Lapwing - below.

Woodlark.

'...they fed close to us, creeping among the cut twigs confident in their camouflage. The male hopped up onto a larger branch and began to sing, then was away high above our heads singing 'lude-de- lude-de lu' displaying a characteristic short tail...'

Piper's Wait

'...As the name suggests, this is a spot to sit and wait. Then perhaps; a goshawk will fill the sky with its powerful form, a red kite will drift by, buzzards will climb on invisible thermals, a woodlark's song will carry on the air or swallows will appear briefly, raising our spirits, then moving en-route to their summer homes...'

Cuckooflower, milkmaids, lady's-smock. Many names for a pretty spring flower. Favoured foodplant of orange tip butterfly larva - right. Creeping willow - bottom right. Hard fern - below.

WINDY - SWALLOWS SWEEPING IN ACROSS PIPSES WAIT - 13th APRIL 2014

Swallows - opposite.
Goshawk - top left.
Red kite - left.
Wren singing his socks off - above.

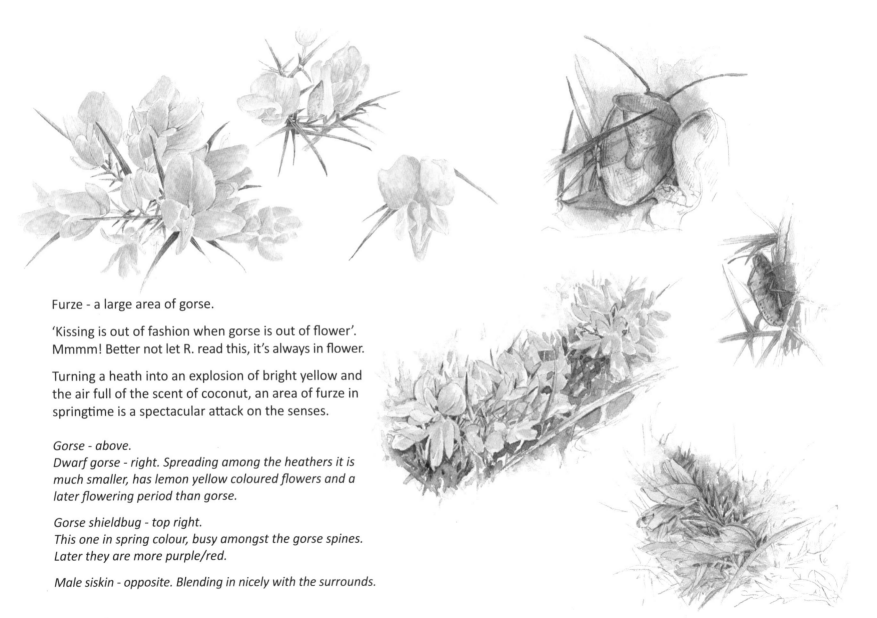

Furze - a large area of gorse.

'Kissing is out of fashion when gorse is out of flower'.
Mmmm! Better not let R. read this, it's always in flower.

Turning a heath into an explosion of bright yellow and
the air full of the scent of coconut, an area of furze in
springtime is a spectacular attack on the senses.

Gorse - above.
Dwarf gorse - right. Spreading among the heathers it is
much smaller, has lemon yellow coloured flowers and a
later flowering period than gorse.

Gorse shieldbug - top right.
This one in spring colour, busy amongst the gorse spines.
Later they are more purple/red.

Male siskin - opposite. Blending in nicely with the surrounds.

DAN POWELL

Butterflies of early spring.

'...a special time, full of treats and expectations. Maybe because they are a welcome splash of colour after the dull winter months, spring butterflies and flowers seem to have the brightest of colours.

My first glimpse of an orange tip - once called 'lady of the woods' is one such treat. The males flit tirelessly around showing off their brilliant orange tips, searching for a mate. Females are more elusive, swopping orange for grey, tucking themselves away in bushes. The intricate mossy patterning on the underside of the hindwing in both sexes provides perfect camouflage when resting...'

Orange tips on ragged robin. Comma and common dog violets. Speckled wood and wood anemone - left to right.

'...A speckled wood's yellow spots shine out as it basks in a ray of sunlight among the white wood anemones...'

Spring to Summer

All roads lead to Hyde Common

'A watched marsh violet never flowers'. A new old country saying.

'...A conversation with an 'eminent' County naturalist went along the lines of. "Marsh violet? We have that at Hyde Common". "When does it flower"? "A bit later than other violets, May to July". Great, piece of cake, it's only a small site, bound to see it........six visits, a payday loan to cover petrol costs later and we had amassed views of; leaves, more leaves, bigger leaves, buds, more buds and finally, cue fanfare....seeds! Not one single flower what-so-ever...'

Adding insult to injury, we found our own marsh violets out in late september, near to Eyeworth Pond. And there in all their glory were; leaves, buds and seeds.

'It seemed so surpassingly lovely - so like a dream of some heavenly country'.

W.H.Hudson - Hampshire Days (1874).

These sketches of marsh violet will be scattered throughout this chapter to denote the stage of growth it was at on that particular day.

And so our spring and summer of 2015 was to be defined by green. However all was not wasted. In creating more and more tenuous routes to arrive at Hyde Common, we went to other places, where the flora and fauna was less reluctant to reveal itself. More about the wildlife of Hyde Common another time, when it's less painful to think about.

Orange tip, ransoms and bluebells - opposite.

Denny Wood

A beautiful open woodland, ancient beech and oak trees.

'...the sun on our backs. The soft notes of a calling buzzard drift across the tree canopy.
A redstart's scratchy song adds to the moment. A brimstone's acid yellow wings flash over
the litter of last autumn's leaves. A cuckoo rests quietly on a dead beech tree. Stock doves call.
Perhaps spring has arrived at last...'

Brimstone - top left. Wood anemone - bottom left & top right.

*Butcher's broom - above. An indicator of ancient woodland.
This strong, spikey evergreen shrub made it ideal for cleaning
butcher's slabs. To look at you wouldn't think that it belongs
to the lily family.*

Fallow bucks - opposite. Stock dove - right.

A lizard basks in the leaf litter - above.
A secretive hawfinch poses just for a moment - left.
A nuthatch calling - below.

Fallow faces and a fallow buck snoozes - opposite.
A cuckoo resting quietly - opposite top.

DAURWELL

Redstart. '...not the most tuneful song rises from the highest beech top and a quivering rusty coloured tail glimpsed can only mean one thing....they're back. Redstarts like swallows are totem birds for us, their arrival lifts our spirits and an hour or so with them can wipe away the doldrums. They are also very smart birds to watch and the desire to paint them is strong. I suspect I have more paintings of redstart than any other bird of the Forest...'

'...Ostentatious. Feeding forays out in the bracken. Tree hole nests. Bright white forehead. Pom-pom chicks. And then they melt away into the woods...'

The tawny owl.

'...R. spotted a large brown bird slaloming low through the beeches, must have been an owl. A family of mistle thrushes had also spotted it and a raucous chorus of rasping clicks ensued, leaving an aural trail of breadcrumbs for us to follow. They led us to a beech tree with the perfect hole for an owl to roost in and sure enough tucked serenely away from the fussing thrushes sat Wally (yes, it had to be named). Eventually the cacophony died down and the thrushes went about their normal business, leaving us with the chance to study Wally at leisure. The owl became a fixture of our visits to Denny W. over the following year, we even had to drop by and wish it a Merry Christmas. Intriguingly the hole has been empty of late, begging the question. Where's Wally?...'

The familiar nocturnal haunting hoot gives away the presence of a tawny owl, yet they are tricky to see, even when they call in the daylight. The best chance of locating one is when, like these mistle thrushes, a group of small birds gather to mob a resting owl, making its life a misery. Fair enough when dusk comes, they are part of the owl's menu.

Above is the small study for the painting on the right.

Silver-washed fritillary. The largest of our fritillaries.

'...in the shade of the woods, following these active butterflies can be quite frustrating as they flap and glide over quite long distances. When they finally come to rest, the beautiful bold markings of the upperwings and the delicate silver-green washes on the underside can be fully appreciated.

However, the presence of blackberry blossom along a woodland ride is irresistible to them...'

Rosemary Watts

38

Standing Hat

Hat - an isolated wood.

Our main reason for dropping by here, is to walk the rides of Pignal Inclosure seeking out pearl-bordered fritillary. It also offers the chance to catch up with a few other spring risers.

Broad-bodied and four-spotted chaser perch up, some making a first landing after emerging from a nearby pond earlier that morning. When they emerge dragonflies are soft-bodied and vulnerable to being attacked by other hardened dragons or worse scoffed by a spider or opportunistic duck. Their best tactic therefore is to get away from the pond and find a safe place to mature.

Flying low over the ground, a small furry bear of a fly with an improbably long proboscis, can only be a bee-fly. Always busy, their friendly demeanour disguises the fact that are a parasite of wasps and some bees. They always make us smile when we see them though.

Pearl-bordered fritillaries feeding on bugle - opposite.
Treecreeper - above.
Four-spotted chaser - top right. Dark-edged bee-fly - right.

Pearl-bordered fritillary. The earliest of our fritillaries to emerge.

They are one of our most endangered species of butterfly, but thanks to the efforts of keepers and the Forestry Commission working to ensure their particular habitat needs are met, they are currently beginning to thrive again.

'...we were lucky enough to watch over a hundred individuals along the rides, feeding on dog violet and bugle (food plants), along with any other plant in flower at the time...'

Fritillaries of the Forest.

Underside patterns of; small pearl-bordered, pearl-bordered, dark green, Glanville and silver-washed - clockwise from top left.

Glanville fritillary.

"This Fly took its Name from the ingenious Lady Glanvil, whose Memory had like to have suffered for her Curiosity. Some Relations that was disappointed by her Will, attempted to let it aside by Acts of Lunacy, for they suggested that none but those who were deprived of their Senses, would go in Pursuit of Butterflies".

Moses Harris - The Aurelian (1766).

No hope for us then.

Ashley Walk

A more remote part in the north of the Forest and another choice mooching area.
Because of its remoteness Ashley Walk became a bombing range in WWII. Many types of
bomb were tested here on various targets, some marked out in chalk brought in from chalk
downland. This explains the presence of early gentian, a chalkland flower discovered growing
here post war.

'...We had been searching unsuccessfully for the early gentians. When out of the corner of
my eye a long tail flicks untidily into the gorse, a scolding rasp follows chastising our unwanted
encroachment into an unmarked territory. We back slowly away and immediately
a handsome male Dartford warbler pops out of the yellow gorse – a New Forest icon.
Of course we had inadvertently ventured too close to its nest and were quite rightly told-off.
From our new acceptable position we were treated to prolonged views of both a male and
female busily foraging for food for their youngsters – mainly small bright green caterpillars.
Reluctantly we left the Dartfords to go about their business and we resumed our search...'

Thyme - left.
Pale dog-violet - right.

'...Cuckoo receiving a bundle of grief from a pair of stonechats and a tree pipit. One of the stonechats landed on the cuckoo's back while it was flying. I suspect that their vexed behaviour was a little too late and the deed was already done...' - above.

Spotted flycatcher seated in holly - right.

Dartford warbler. The Forest supports a nationally important population of this resident warbler. They are susceptible to very cold winters, therefore a ready supply of spiders and insect larva is essential to their survival.

Dockens Water at Holly Hatch

Holly Hatch Inclosure created whilst Napoleon waged war in Europe. Hatch - a gateway.

'...To recover from another failed violet visit, we took a wander along Dockens Water at Holly H. Keeping to the shady edge of the stream we were pleased to note three spotted flyctacher territories (an increasingly hard bird to find), along with blackcaps, willow warblers, chiffchaff and a stunning male bullfinch pulling goat willow seeds apart. Conspicuous by their absence were dragons, at a time of year like this, the Water should be alive with sparring beasts - the cold conditions of this spring had obviously worked against them this year. Dragons need it warm, as do we...'

Bullfinch - left.
Cow-wheat and yellow pimpernel - above.

Cadnam Stream

'...Optimistic that this would be the day that the violet would be a show of flowery colour, we set off for Hyde Common. First we dropped by the small bridge near to Cadnam Common to see ivy-leaved bellflower. It was out in abundance, the omens for the day were looking good. R. went into painting mode. I started snooping about and almost immediately a freshly emerged white admiral appeared and just as quickly disappeared again. A short search ensued and it was refound, resting in an apple tree. Over the next twenty minutes it flitted between trees and bracken, before deciding that we had bothered it enough and retreated to the canopy. Onward to Hyde and violet glory.....we wish! The highlight of the rest of the day was a scrummy bacon butty at the nearby Hyde tearoom...'

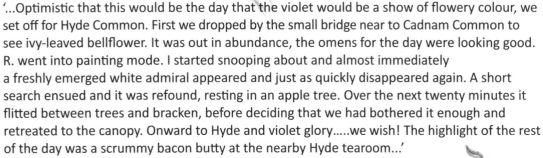

Ivy-leaved bellflower.

'...It took us a couple of attempts to find this beautiful little flower, mainly because we were looking in the wrong place. A pale blue hue to the mossy cushions on the damp edges of the stream told us we were finally in the right place. The delicate flowers and soft colours were difficult to resist, so I didn't and soon I set myself to studying it in more detail...'

White admiral. Although spending much of their time in the tree canopy, their black and white markings and distinctive gliding flight make them one of the easier butterflies to identify.

'London vomits out its annual crowd of collectors'. W.H.Hudson (1903).

During Victorian times the Forest in summer swarmed with insects, which in turn beckoned insect collectors to gather in their swarms. Their arrival in the summer provided a welcome boost to the local economy. Butterflies were most popular; fritillaries, white admiral and purple emperor in particular were "taken" in their thousands.

Lost Forest butterflies. Rare species like; wood white, large tortoiseshell, Camberwell beauty and high brown fritillary once graced the Forest. Sadly no longer.

We had to travel to Exmoor to see this high brown fritillary. It was once more abundant in the Forest than dark green fritillary. The last records were from 1983. These days more sympathetic management is being employed. Let's hope this magnificent butterfly will make a comeback.

Green-veined white and foxglove - right.
Hornet and hoverfly - above.
Chiffchaff in blossom - opposite.

Beaulieu Road Station

Bishop's Dyke. It is not really known how the dyke was created, but a fanciful theory goes. "The New Forest peasant will tell that this was a grant of land as much as the Bishop of Winchester could in a day crawl round on his hands and knees". John Wise in the nineteenth century.

'...Oddly quiet for the time of year. On a hot day like this, Bishop's D. should have been alive with dragons and birds, instead there was little to discover. Except for a confiding kingfisher that accompanied us in our failed search for various bladderworts. In turn he was accompanied by a reed bunting and stonechat.

Crossing under the railway line; a meadow pipit called loudly, anxiously leading us away from its nest, young Dartfords flicked around a small silver birch and a toadlet did its best not to be stamped on - successfully...' Maybe not so quiet after all.

Meadow pipit in the pink - above.
Kingfisher and reed bunting. Toadlet - opposite.

Kingfisher. Also known as halcyon, an idyllic name. Normally views in the Forest are limited to flashes of blue disappearing around the meander of a small stream. The opportunity to share time at leisure with such a stunningly coloured bird was eagerly grasped. Halcyon days indeed.

Some orchids of the Forest

Ranging from the modest bog orchid, when you can stand in a bog, staring for an age at one spot slowly sinking into the mire before seeing one. To the delicate heath-spotted orchid, that can decorate a heath in their hundreds and the elegance of the subtle lesser butterfly orchid.

Bog, green-winged, early marsh, lesser butterfly,
southern marsh and heath-spotted - left to right.

FOREST WARCASES - BALLILLA COMMON AUG '19
DAN POWELL

Summer

Bramshaw Commons

Found among the woodlands and heaths are the commons and village greens of the Forest. Trampled and short cropped by livestock and ponies, they appear bland and devoid of much interest. But they are special places that support a wide variety of uncommon plants, including; chamomile, pennyroyal and small fleabane. All have their strongholds in the Forest.

In the past traditional village greens with grazing livestock and carts that churned up muddy ruts, were full of small fleabane and pennyroyal. Many have given way to tidy manicured lawns, where uninteresting grasses grow. Today the Forest commons and greens are precious habitats for these rare flowers.

'...The commons in summer have an air of tranquility and timelessness about them. We both quickly relax and settle into sketchy mode. R. getting into the flowers found in the damp shallow hollows, along with the pigs and wonky donkeys eating their way around the green. Me, enjoying the swallows that feed on flies that gather around the munchers' droppings...'

On a few occasions wheatears have stopped by on their journey south to warmer climes, also attracted to the flies.

Munchers at work - opposite and right.

Flowers of the commons.

Chamomile is a nationally scarce flower, but here in the Forest it thrives. On a warm summers day there is nothing like walking over a chamomile lawn, releasing aromatic scent into the air.

Small fleabane is not a showy little plant and can be easily overlooked. Its characteristics give it a weedy feel. Botonists love it.

Pennyroyal grows in damp ditches or around the edges of pools. A creeping plant with lovely soft mauve flowers, growing in whorls.

Chamomile, small water-pepper, trifid bur-marigold, lesser fleabane & pennyroyal - left to right.

60

Rosemary Wells

Hatchet to Crockford

Hatchet Pond. Created in the 18th century to provide power for an iron mill.

'...Blarsted heath. The hottest day of the year and we decide to walk across Beaulieu Heath from Hatchet Pond to Crockford Bridge and back again. A little look in a bog, a stroll out on heath and lawn, a mooch along the stream, ending with a cool pint of bitter at the Turfcutters...'

Dark green fritillary - opposite. A butterfly of the open heath.
A knapped flint tool - below. Found on the heath, the nearby Bronze Age barrows hint at the age of the hand that created it.

Bog plants.
Insectivorous plants. Lesser bladderwort - top. Pale butterwort - below. Bladderworts have underwater bristly bladders and butterworts sticky leaves and flowers, that entrap their prey.
Bog pimpernel - right.

Silver-studded blue. The heaths are a stronghold for this small pretty butterfly. The silver studs can be seen on the underside of the rear wing. On a warm sunny day they can flutter in their hundreds over the heather, the males flashing bright blue wings.

They have a close relationship with species of black ant, who play a vital role through their life-cycle. The caterpillars are taken into the ants' nest and raised by them, thinking they are their own. Even as the adult butterfly emerges, it will have several ants in attendance, attracted by drops of liquid secreted from the abdomen. This gives the butterfly protection during the vulnerable period as the wings harden.

'...The male posed nicely on the bogside bracken, sometimes dropping to the floor and walking around rubbing its hindwings together in an awkward manner - maybe to attract ants?...'

'...Out on the picture calendar heath, it was clear that this was going to be a grayling day, in the end counted over a hundred during our walk. The heather was flickering with movement, flashes of ochre colour, gliding on stiff upturned wings, flick-flick-glide. Easy to follow while they fly, as soon they land not so. When landed the wings might be slightly open, offering a glimpse of bright yellow/ochre and a deep brown eye, then in an instant the wings are closed and the butterfly has melted away - secure that their cryptic markings have merged with the background.

We watched as a female started to egg-lay. An ungainly affair that involved much twitching and fussing about, culminating with her raising her body handstand-like on her forelegs and then slowly lowering her abdomen onto an approved stem to deposit her egg...'

Now you see me - left. Now you don't - above.

Six-spot burnet - top. Also out in force this day.

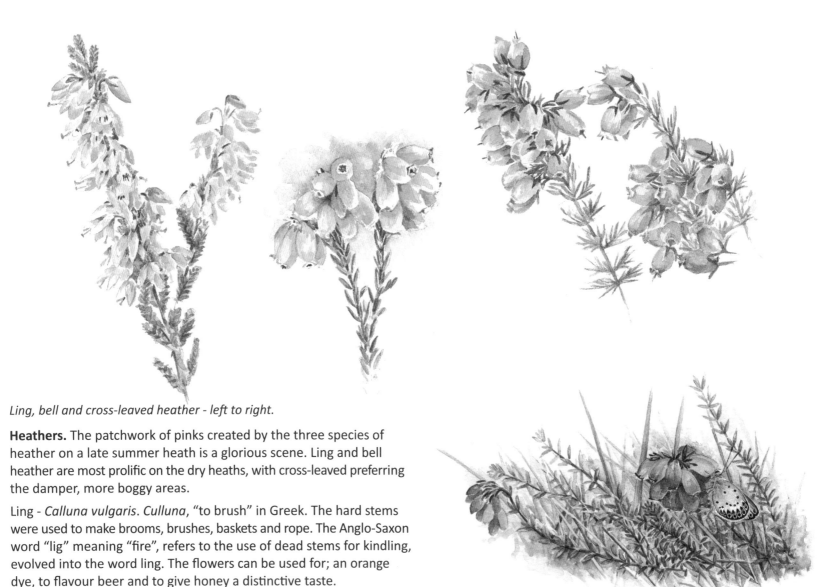

Ling, bell and cross-leaved heather - left to right.

Heathers. The patchwork of pinks created by the three species of heather on a late summer heath is a glorious scene. Ling and bell heather are most prolific on the dry heaths, with cross-leaved preferring the damper, more boggy areas.

Ling - *Calluna vulgaris*. *Culluna*, "to brush" in Greek. The hard stems were used to make brooms, brushes, baskets and rope. The Anglo-Saxon word "lig" meaning "fire", refers to the use of dead stems for kindling, evolved into the word ling. The flowers can be used for; an orange dye, to flavour beer and to give honey a distinctive taste.

'...model aircraft buzzed, playing out noisy dogfights. A Dartford warbler called, teased, showing briefly, then not, then popped out onto a gorse stem, began preening and was gone again.
A small group of skylark flew ahead, leading our way...'

Stonechat - left. The guardians of the heath.
Dartfords - above. Painted lady - below.

'...the heady aroma of bog myrtle in the air told us we were finally at Crockford Bridge. Superb for flora, invertebrates and hot artists...'

Purple hairstreak - above. Often seen flicking manically around the tops of the oak trees by Crockford car park.
Golden-ringed dragonfly - right. The masters of the stream.

Opposite. Beautiful demoiselle - far left. The dandies of the stream.

Pillwort with pills - middle top. A rare fern. Hampshire purslane - middle bottom. Forms deep red mats over wet areas. Lesser water plantain - top right. All three have their strongholds in the Forest.

Aquarius paludum - bottom left. A giant of a pondskater.

Marsh gentian

'...carrying on to Steephill Bottom to seek out this fabulous ultramarine trumpet of a flower. We soon spotted their beautiful blue shapes tucked in among the pinks of the damper heath - a colour combination not to be resisted.

I settled down to sketch them, but with dark clouds looming we soon had to head for cover from the inevitable downpour. Back at my flower I found that the cold and rain had caused it to close. However I cupped it in my hands and the warmth gradually helped it to spiral open again, allowing me to complete my paintings...'

The gentian is able to cope with growing among the heather, but is susceptible to being overshadowed by large mature plants. To prevent this the heather is periodically burnt back, allowing the gentian space to regenerate. It can take up to three years before they flower again, but when they do it can be in big numbers - on this day we counted over eighty.

Betony - top. Lesser centaury - above.
Marsh gentian - left.

Pannage. The Forest is one of the few places in Britain where pigs are turned out in pannage.

'...Pigs? What can I say about them? They are brilliant. Apart from providing me hours of fun to watch and draw, they also have a special job to do. During the autumn they are allowed to wander the woods to feed on acorns, which are harmful to cattle and ponies. They also hoover up any other fruits that take their fancy, let's face it they'll eat almost anything...'

Autumn to Winter

'...A female brimstone, flew through the woods...'

Eyeworth Pond to Leaden Hall and back.

'...The chance to see ring ouzels at Leaden Hall was too tempting to ignore. We could have parked close to the site, but being us we parked miles away at Eyeworth Pond to make a day of it. Having said hello to the pigs, we wandered through the woods, watching nuthatches, treecreepers and as D. says "where there's holly, a firecrest won't be far away" and it wasn't. And of course we couldn't ignore the fungi, which remained unidentified as usual.

Onto the heath, we eventually arrived at the ouzels, having seen; wheatear, Dartford warbler meadow pipit and skylark...'

Fungi. Not just for autumn, but for all seasons.
The nutrient recycling system is down to fungi, they are the "waste management and disposal technicians" of the woodland. Breaking down; fallen leaves, wood, dung and dead matter. Without them life in the Forest would quickly fall apart - if we don't want to lose them, we really ought to stop "collecting" them in the numbers that we do.

Some 2,600 species have been recorded in the Forest alone.....it would be nice to be able to name some! Seven books bought, pages of sketches made, a hard drive packed with photos and they are still a complete mystery to us. Yet failing to put a name to the majority of them hasn't detracted from our enjoyment of the good, the bad and the downright ugly of the fungi world.

'...The ring ouzels were in an unusually showy mood, the berries of the whitebeam proving irresistible, a captivating combination for D. to paint. In recent years Leaden H. has become a regular stopping off point for this shy mountain thrush. Today we saw two young males. At other times there have been over ten.

Sketches made and a chinwag with friends, it was time to make our way back. Darkness came quickly and we didn't exactly retrace our steps...'

'...Smart birds, white bibs, scaly plumage, chacking calls, berries - equals happy chappy...'

Spotted flycatcher and hawthorn berries - opposite.

Winter

HARRIER ROOST   BLACK GUTTER BOTTOM
JAN 15TH '05

Black Gutter Bottom

A gutter is a small stream that runs through a valley bottom.

Roosting hen harriers. When the day trippers have left for home and the light has almost slipped over the horizon, you might just witness something magical.

Acknowledgements

This is our first solo flight in publishing, so please be gentle with us if you find any mishaps.

To our families for their continued support, patience and encouragement in our mad choice for making a living. Thank you.

Cheers to all our friends. Especially Mike and Jan for learning us to write good. Aimée and Pete for leading the way and bringing doughnuts.

Thanks to Nigel Ede for your vision, you are missed. To Tony Norris for being a friend, champion of our work and writing such an eloquent foreword.

References

Chatters, C (2009) Flowers of the Forest. Wildguides. Still my favourite toilet read.
Thomas, J & Lewington, R (2010) The Butterflies of Britain and Ireland. British wildlife Publishing.
Brock, P (2011) Insects of the New Forest. Piscespublications.
British Wildlife Magazine.
www.newforestexplorersguide.co.uk

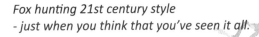

Fox hunting 21st century style
- just when you think that you've seen it all.